BASS

SI ONLINE

Multimedia Resources for
TEACHERS
STUDENTS
PARENTS

SOUND INNOVATIONS

SOUND DEVELOPMENT

Warm-up Exercises for Tone and Technique

INTERMEDIATE STRING ORCHESTRA

Bob **PHILLIPS** | Kirk **MOSS**

Sound Innovations: Sound Development emphasizes playing with a characteristic, beautiful sound through four unique levels. The levels can be used in any order, either as individual warm-ups or structured units, so you can create the best sequence for your development. Video demonstrations, audio accompaniment tracks, and additional supplemental material are included and can be accessed at **SIOnline.alfred.com**.

Level 1: Sound Tone

Develop excellent tone with exercises focusing on bowing lanes, bow weight, and bow speed. Level 1 develops the skills that affect tone production through warm-up exercises that are easy to teach and play.

Level 2: Sound Bowings

This level helps develop right-hand skills. Refine your hooked bowings, articulate martelé and spiccato, and learn collé through a comprehensive presentation of bowing (attack strokes).

Level 3: Sound Shifting

Shifting techniques are introduced through harmonics, and positions are thoroughly presented using finger patterns. The structure of this level facilitates teaching and learning shifting in a heterogeneous class.

Level 4: Sound Scales, Arpeggios, Chorales, and Rhythms

Level 4 allows each section or player to play one or two octaves while the ensemble plays either the same or different octaves. Exercises include scales, arpeggios, broken thirds, accompaniment lines, chorales, and rhythms in a variety of meters.

SI ONLINE

Multimedia Resources for
TEACHERS
STUDENTS
PARENTS

 Audio accompaniment tracks are included for every line of music in the book.

 Video demonstrations of key skills are included. Look for the video icon throughout this book.

 PDF content provides the opportunity to practice scales and arpeggios in all keys.

Visit the *SI Online* resource site to stay up to date with newly added content.
SIOnline.alfred.com

Alfred Music
P.O. Box 10003
Van Nuys, CA 91410-0003
alfred.com

ISBN-10: 0-7390-6805-9 (Book & Online Media)
ISBN-13: 978-0-7390-6805-2 (Book & Online Media)

Instrument photos courtesy of Yamaha Corporation of America Band & Orchestral Division

Level 1: Sound Tone
Bowing Lanes

A **BOWING LANE** is the area between the fingerboard and bridge where the bow is placed:

Pianissimo Lane
Piano Lane
Mezzo Piano Lane
Mezzo Forte Lane
Forte Lane
Fortissimo Lane

E A D G

1 **PLAYING IN THE MEZZO FORTE (*mf*) LANE**—*Place your bow in the mezzo forte (mf) lane slightly toward the bridge.*

mf

2 **PLAYING IN THE FORTE (*f*) LANE**—*Place your bow in the forte (f) lane near the bridge.*

f

TILTING THE STICK

Tilt the stick of the bow by rolling it slightly toward the scroll. Only the edge of the hair will now contact the string.

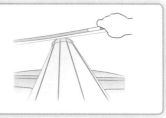

3 **PLAYING IN THE MEZZO PIANO (*mp*) LANE**—*Place your bow in the mezzo piano (mp) lane slightly toward the fingerboard and tilt your bow toward the scroll.*

mp

4 **PLAYING IN THE PIANO (*p*) LANE**—*Place your bow in the piano (p) lane near the fingerboard and tilt the bow stick toward the scroll. Play in the middle section of the bow.*

p

5 **PLAYING IN THE FORTISSIMO (*ff*) LANE**—*Place your bow in the fortissimo (ff) lane very near the bridge and use flat bow hair. Be sure to move the bow slowly and save bow in the last two measures.*

ff

6 **PLAYING IN THE PIANISSIMO (*pp*) LANE**—*Place your bow in the pianissimo (pp) lane very near the fingerboard and tilt your bow stick toward the scroll. Challenge: Perform* Playing in the Fortissimo Lane *and* Playing in the Pianissimo Lane *as one piece.*

pp

Level 1: Sound Tone
Bowing Lanes

> 📹 **PARALLEL BOWING**—Set your bow on the D string at the midpoint of the bow. Push your right hand away from your head and then toward your head in a rowing motion. Pushing your right hand away from you creates an X where the bow hair and the string intersect. Pulling the bow towards you creates an X also. Push or pull the right hand until the bow hair makes a perfect T with the string so it is perpendicular to the string and parallel to the bridge. Keeping the bow perpendicular to the string and parallel to the bridge helps create a beautiful tone.

7 **ROW YOUR BOW**—*Row your bow back and forth during each measure of rest and then stop when it is perpendicular to the string and parallel to the bridge.*

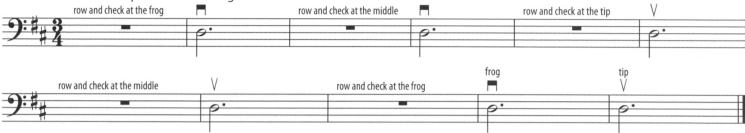

8 **CHANGING BOWING LANES**—*Gradually move the bow from the* pianissimo *(pp) to the* fortissimo *(ff) bowing lane and back. Remember to keep your bow parallel to the bridge. Challenge: Go back and play the exercise starting up bow.*

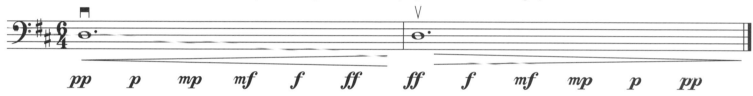

9 **CHANGING BOWING LANES IN ONE BOW**—*Move from the* pianissimo *(pp) to the* fortissimo *(ff) bowing lane and back all in one bow. Remember to keep your bow parallel to the bridge. Challenge: Go back and play the exercise starting up bow.*

10 **THEME FROM SYMPHONY NO. 104, MVT. 4**—*Practice changing from the* mezzo forte *(mf) to the* forte *(f) bowing lane.*

Joseph Haydn

11 **COSSACK LULLABY**—*Practice changing from the* piano *(p) to the* pianissimo *(pp) bowing lane. Compare and contrast the musical elements of* Cossack Lullaby *from the Romantic period of music and* Theme from Symphony No. 104 *from the Classical period of music.*

Russian Folk Song

Level 1: Sound Tone
Bow Weight

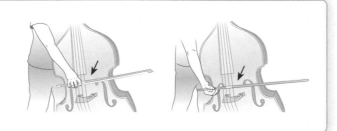

BOW WEIGHT is the amount of pressure applied to the string using the right arm and hand. Weight causes the bow to sink into the string.

12 **MEDIUM-HEAVY BOW WEIGHT**—*Place your bow in the* mezzo forte (*mf*) *lane and play with a medium-heavy amount of arm weight in the bow. Play with flat bow hair. Challenge: Go back and play the exercise in a two-part round (group A and B) as your teacher directs.*

13 **HEAVY BOW WEIGHT**—*Place your bow in the* forte (*f*) *lane and play with a heavy amount of arm weight in the bow. Play with flat bow hair.*

14 **VERY-HEAVY BOW WEIGHT**—*Place your bow in the* fortissimo (*ff*) *lane and play with a very heavy amount of arm weight in the bow. Play with flat bow hair. Be sure to move the bow slowly (save bow) in the last two bars.*

15 **MEDIUM-LIGHT BOW WEIGHT**—*Place your bow in the* mezzo piano (*mp*) *lane and play with a medium-light amount of hand weight in the bow. Play in the middle of the bow. Tilt the bow.*

16 **LIGHT BOW WEIGHT**—*Place your bow in the* piano (*p*) *lane and play with a light amount of hand weight in the bow. Play in the upper half of the bow. Tilt the bow.*

17 **VERY-LIGHT BOW WEIGHT**—*Place your bow in the* pianissimo (*pp*) *lane and play with a very light amount of hand weight in the bow. Play near the tip of the bow. Tilt the bow.*

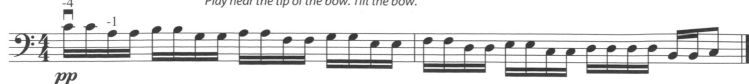

Level 1: Sound Tone
Bow Weight

18 DYNAMIC CONTRAST—*Practice using a heavy bow weight and a light bow weight. Release any tension in your bow-hand fingers during the rests.*

RELEASING BOW WEIGHT EXERCISE
1. Set the middle of the bow on the D string.
2. Transfer your arm weight through your wrist, hand and evenly amongst your fingers.
3. Allow the bow stick to sink toward the string.
4. Release the weight and feel the natural spring of the bow stick.

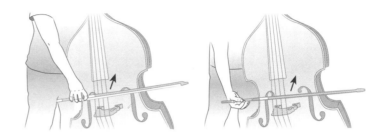

Leopold Mozart (the father of Wolfgang Amadeus Mozart) taught a variation of this exercise in the 18th century. Use bow strokes that change from loud in the first part of the stroke to soft in the second part. See how deeply you can sink the bow into the string without breaking the tone. Feel the give of the wood of the bow, the hair and the string. Avoid an accent, scratch, or bite at the start of the tone.

19 PULSING TONE—*Practice changing from a medium-heavy to a light bow weight while staying in the mezzo forte (**mf**) bowing lane.*

20 DEEP TONE, PULSE TONE—*Practice pulsing the bow.*

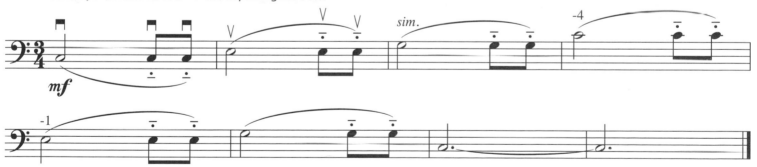

21 FRENCH FOLK SONG—*Practice playing this portion of French Folk Song with three pulses per measure.*
Challenge: Play the rest of the song by ear.

Traditional

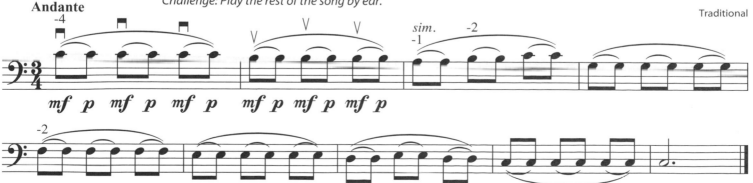

Level 1: Sound Tone
Bow Speed

> **BOW SPEED** is how fast or slow the bow moves across the string. Expressive playing employs a range of bow speeds from very fast to very slow.
>
> **MAELZEL'S METRONOME**, abbreviated M.M., uses a number which indicates the number of beats per minute on the metronome. It is often shown with a note value in place of M.M. (♩ = 80). Use a metronome to keep a steady tempo and play each of the exercises below at (♩ = 80).

22   **MEDIUM-FAST BOW SPEED**—*Place your bow in the* mezzo piano (*mp*) *lane with a medium-light amount of hand weight and move the bow at a medium-fast bow speed.*

23   **MEDIUM-SLOW BOW SPEED**—*Place your bow in the* mezzo forte (*mf*) *lane with a medium-heavy amount of arm weight and move the bow at a medium-slow bow speed.*

24   **SLOW BOW SPEED**—*Place your bow in the* forte (*f*) *lane with a heavy amount of arm weight and move the bow at a slow bow speed.*

25   **VERY-SLOW BOW SPEED**—*Place your bow in the* fortissimo (*ff*) *lane with a very-heavy amount of arm weight and move the bow at a very-slow bow speed. Challenge: Play this piece slurring four measures in one bow.*

26   **FAST BOW SPEED**—*Place your bow in the* piano (*p*) *lane, play with a light amount of hand weight and move the bow at a fast bow speed. Play in the middle of the bow.*

27   **VERY-FAST BOW SPEED**—*Place your bow in the* pianissimo (*pp*) *lane, play with a very-light amount of hand weight and move the bow at a very-fast bow speed. Play near the tip of the bow.*

Level 1: Sound Tone
Bow Speed

28 **CHANGING FROM SLOW TO FAST BOW SPEED**—*Move the bow slowly on the first three beats of each measure with a medium bow weight. Each 4th beat will be played with a fast bow speed. The up bow will travel in one beat as far as the down bow travels in three beats.*

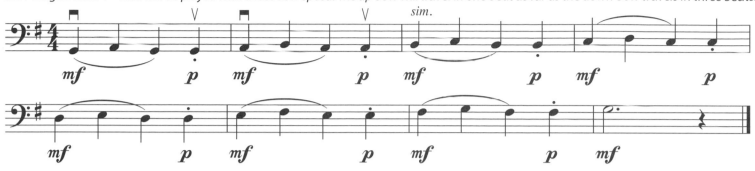

29 **CHANGING FROM FAST TO SLOW BOW SPEED**—*Move the bow quickly on beat 1 of each measure with a light bow weight. Each down bow will last one beat while the up bow will travel the same distance in three beats.*

30 **SAVE AND SPEND THE BOW**—*Play the first three beats using only 1/3 of the bow and beat 4 using the remaining 2/3.*

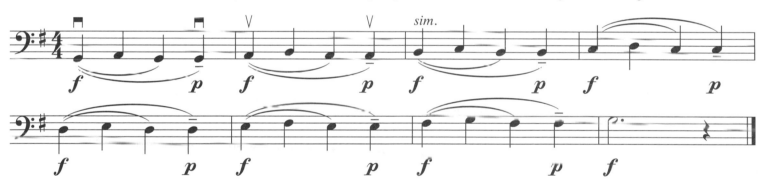

 USING DIFFERENT PARTS OF THE BOW

The whole bow can be divided into three parts: the *lower* third, the *middle* third and the *upper* third.

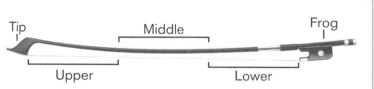

31 **SAKURA**—*Practice playing at the tip, upper third, middle third, lower third and frog of the bow. On the measures marked crawl, use a faster bow speed to move to a different part of the bow.*

Japanese Folk Song

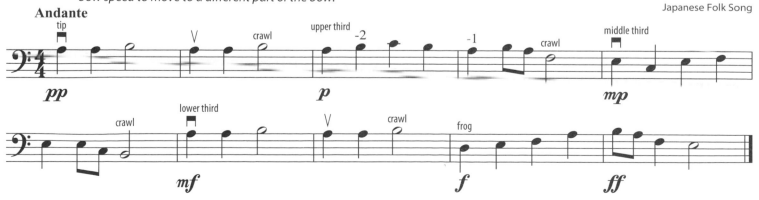

Level 1: Sound Tone
Bow Division

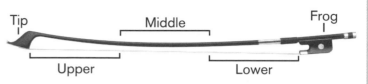

USING DIFFERENT PARTS OF THE BOW

The whole bow can be divided into three parts:
the *lower* third, the *middle* third and the *upper* third.

32 **PLAYING IN THE UPPER THIRD**—*Play the entire line in the upper third of the bow.*

Rodolphe Kreutzer

33 **PLAYING IN THE MIDDLE THIRD**—*Play the entire line in the middle third of the bow.*

34 **PLAYING IN THE LOWER THIRD**—*Play the entire line in the lower third of the bow.*

35 **MOVING FROM FROG TO TIP**—*Start in the lower third of the bow and gradually crawl to the upper third of the bow.*

lower third   middle third   upper third

36 **MOVING FROM TIP TO FROG**—*Start in the upper third of the bow and gradually crawl to the lower third of the bow.*

upper third   middle third   lower third

37 **PLAYING WITH A WHOLE BOW**—*Use a whole bow on each note. Be sure to move the bow slowly (save bow) in the last measure.*
Challenge: Go back and play the entire page as one piece.

Level 1: Sound Tone
Tone Repertoire

38 **THE GREAT GATE OF KIEV**—*Start in the* forte *(f) lane with a heavy bow weight moving at a slow speed. Adjust the tone variables as needed throughout the piece. Then describe the adjustments you made. Listen to a recording of a professional performance of this piece and analyze how the players control the tone variables when they play.*

Modest Mussorgsky

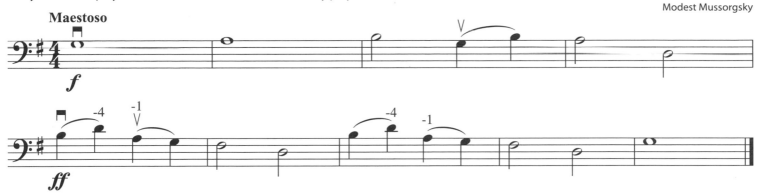

39 **THEME FROM SYMPHONY NO. 1**—*Start in the* mezzo forte *(mf) lane with a medium-heavy bow weight moving at medium-slow speed. Adjust the tone variables as needed throughout the piece. Then describe the adjustments you made. Listen to a professional recording of this piece and compare your performance to it.*

Johannes Brahms

40 **ARIRANG**—*Start in the* pianissimo *(pp) lane with a very-light bow weight moving at a very-fast speed. Adjust the tone variables as needed throughout the piece. How does adjusting tone variables compare to the use of color in the visual arts?*

Korean Folk Song

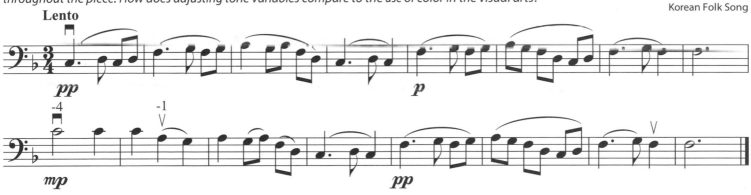

41 **CRIPPLE CREEK**—*Start in the* mezzo forte *lane with a medium-weight bow moving at a medium-slow speed. Adjust the tone variables as needed throughout the piece. Then describe the adjustments you made.*

American Fiddle Tune

Challenge 1: Listen to each piece of music above and decide the style and which historical period it's from.
Challenge 2: Use the tone variables you have learned in Level 1 to play songs from various cultures and time periods
that you learned in Sound Innovations books 1 and 2.

Level 2: Sound Bowings
Detaché

DETACHÉ—Separate bow strokes played smoothly with an eveness of tone. *Sound Advice:* Keep the bow parallel to the bridge.

 BOW WRITING EXERCISE
1. Hold the bow in a vertical position.
2. While sitting, lean forward and rest your right forearm on your leg.
3. Allow your right wrist to extend past your knee.
4. Pretend the adjusting screw of the bow is a pencil.
5. Use the flexible joints in the wrist, fingers, and thumb to write your signature in the air.
6. Avoid tilting the stick as you write.

(Watch video for German bow)

DETACHÉ BOWING ABOVE AND BELOW THE MIDDLE OF THE BOW
Move your right arm smoothly by using a flexible elbow.

42 PAVANNE—*Start in the piano (**p**) lane with a light bow weight and a medium-fast bow speed. Move your right arm smoothly to create a beautiful detaché stroke.*

French Renaissance Dance

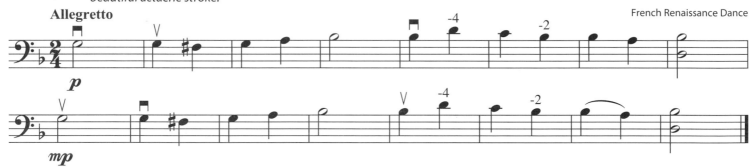

DETACHÉ BOWING USING HAND AND WRIST MOVEMENT
Move your bow smoothly by using your wrist and fingers.

HAND AND WRIST MOVEMENT EXERCISE
1. Hold your right hand loosely in front of you.
2. Let your right-hand fingers dangle.
3. Use your right hand as if it is a paint brush and paint your music stand.
4. Let your right-hand fingers move back and forth like the bristles on the brush.

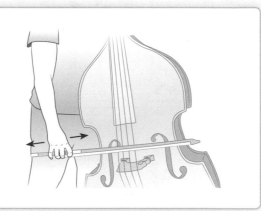

43 CREDO FROM MASS NO. 2, EXCERPT 1—*Start in the mezzo forte (**mf**) lane with a medium-heavy bow weight and a fast bow speed. Use a flexible wrist and fingers to play a detaché stroke on each eighth note.*

Franz Schubert

Level 2: Sound Bowings
Tremolo

TREMOLO–Separate bow strokes played as quickly as possible. *Sound Advice:* Play near the tip for softer dynamic levels.

44 **PLAYING TREMOLO**—*Starting in the upper part of the bow accelerate the bow speed through each measure until you are playing* tremolo *in measure 4.*

45 **THEME OF THE BAD GUYS**—*Start in the piano* (***p***) *lane with a light bow weight and move the bow as quickly as possible for the* tremolo. *Change the bowing lanes and crawl the bow as needed. Describe what you changed.*

STACCATO–Bow strokes that stop and release the sound after each note creating a separation or space between notes. *Sound Advice:* Keep the bow weight even through the note.

46 **LEARNING TO PLAY STACCATO**—*Practice going from* detaché *to staccato* bowing in the middle third of the bow.

47 **CREDO FROM MASS NO. 2, EXCERPT 2**—*Practice playing* staccato *in the lower third of the bow.*

Franz Schubert

Level 2: Sound Bowings
Staccato Hooks

STACCATO HOOKS—Two or more stopped strokes that are played in the same bow direction and are usually notated with slurs. *Sound Advice:* Each note should have a bell tone that rings and then decays.

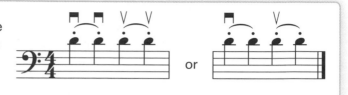

48 **LEARNING TO PLAY STACCATO HOOKS**—*Starting in the lower third of the bow, be careful to stop the bow and release the sound after each staccato note.*

49 **PLAYING STACCATO HOOKS**—*Starting in the lower third of the bow, practice playing staccato hooks.*

50 **PACK SHE BACK TO SHE MA**—*Starting in the lower third of the bow, practice playing staccato hooks. Challenge: Circle the staccato hooked notes.*

Barbados Folk Song

51 **CABBAGE AND BEETS**—*Starting in the lower third of the bow, be careful to stop the bow, and release the sound after each staccato note.*

German Folk Song

52 **NON PIÙ ANDRAI**—*Starting in the middle third of the bow, practice playing staccato hooked bowings. Be careful to play the rhythms accurately.*

Wolfgang Amadeus Mozart

Level 2: Sound Bowings
Legato Hooks

TENUTO—To hold a note for its full value, indicated by a line over or under the note.

LEGATO HOOKS—Two or more legato strokes played in the same bow direction called **PORTATO (LOURÉ)**.
Sound Advice: Each note should have a pulsed tone.

53 LEARNING TO PLAY LEGATO HOOKS—*Be careful to play smoothly.*

54 ALLEGRO CON BRIO FROM SYMPHONY NO. 1—*Practice playing legato hooked quarter notes.*

Ludwig van Beethoven

55 PLAYING LEGATO HOOKED EIGHTH NOTES—*Practice playing legato hooked eighth notes.*

56 THEME FROM KEYBOARD CONCERTO—*Play using legato hooked bowings.*

Johann Sebastian Bach

Level 2: Sound Bowings
Martelé

MARTELÉ

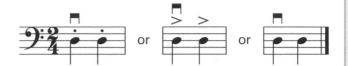

MARTELÉ—Separate bow strokes that start with weight in the bow to create a crisp attack. The weight is partially released as the note starts. The bow stops and releases the sound at the end of the note. *Sound Advice:* Use heavy-light bow weight and fast-slow bow speed.

STRING WIGGLE EXERCISE—Pinch the bow into the string so the hair grips the string and wiggles it, silently pulling the string from side to side (   ). Feel the spring in the bow stick.

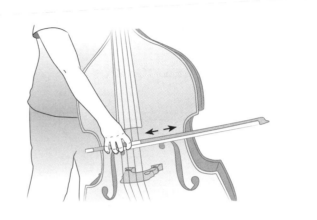

THE CLICK EXERCISE—Play *martelé* with a fast-slow bow speed. Release the pressure (weight) the instant the bow moves and listen for the "click" at the beginning.

57 **LEARNING TO PLAY MARTELÉ**—*During each rest, wiggle the string back and forth using flexible fingers on the bow. Use the* martelé *stroke on each quarter note.*

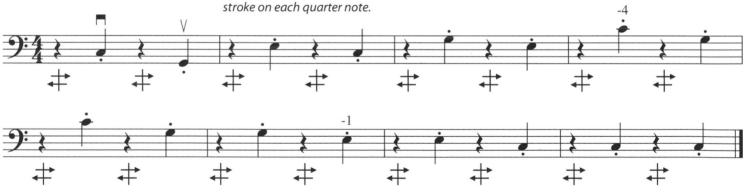

58 **PLAYING MARTELÉ ON TWO QUARTER NOTES**—*During each rest, wiggle the string back and forth using flexible fingers on the bow. Use the* martelé *stroke on each quarter note.*

Level 2: Sound Bowings
Martelé

59 **PLAYING MARTELÉ ON THE C SCALE**—*Practice using the martelé bow stroke on each note of the C scale in the middle of the bow.*
Challenge: Play this exercise using different dynamic levels and sections of the bow.

60 **BRITISH GRENADIERS**—*Start in the forte (𝆑) lane with heavy bow weight and use the martelé bow stroke in the middle of the bow.*

English Folk Song

61 **LEARNING TO PLAY WITH A FAST MARTELÉ**—*Start in the piano (𝒑) lane using the upper third of the bow with a light bow weight moving the bow very fast on each eighth note.*

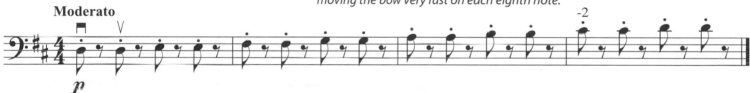

62 **PLAYING WITH A FAST MARTELÉ ON EIGHTH NOTES**—*Start in the mezzo piano (𝒎𝒑) lane using the upper third of the bow with a medium-light bow weight and move the bow very fast on each eighth note.*

63 **GLORIA**—*Play martelé by starting in the middle of the bow in the mezzo piano (𝒎𝒑) lane with a medium-light bow weight and move the bow very fast on each eighth note. Listen to a professional recording of this piece and develop a musical checklist to compare and evaluate your performance.*

Antonio Vivaldi

Level 2: Sound Bowings
Collé

COLLÉ—A sharply pinched-attack bow stroke that is lifted off the string in a scoop motion, sometimes called a bowed pizzicato. *Sound Advice:* Use finger action to lift and set the bow.

BOW PULL-UP EXERCISE
1. Hold the bow in a vertical position.
2. While sitting, lean forward and rest your right forearm on your leg.
3. Allow your wrist to extend past your knee.
4. Use finger action to pull the bow half an inch upward. Notice how the knuckles bend and fingers curve.
5. Return the bow downward to its starting point. Notice how the fingers straighten.
6. Repeat this motion several times.

FROG AND TIP COLLÉ

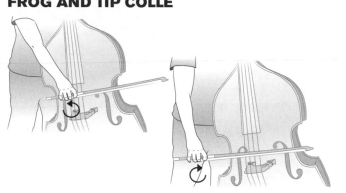

64 **COLLÉ EXERCISE**—*During the first rest, set/pinch the bow into the string in the lower third of the bow. Wiggle the string with the bow and then flick the bow off the string.*

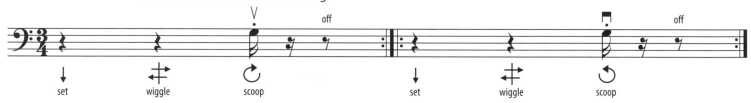

65 **PLAYING REPEATED COLLÉ BOW STROKES**—*Reset the bow after each sixteenth note.*

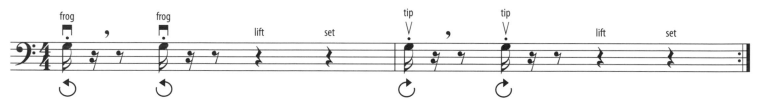

66 **CHANGING ENDS OF THE BOW**—*After each set of down or up bows, move to the opposite end of the bow during the rests.*

67 **CHANGING ENDS OF THE BOW ON THE D SCALE**—*After each set of down or up bows, move to the opposite end of the bow during the rests.*

Level 2: Sound Bowings
Collé

68 **PLAYING THE D SCALE USING COLLÉ**—*During the rests between sixteenth notes, lift the bow to the opposite end and prepare to play.*
Challenge: Reverse the bowings starting up bow at the frog and down bow at the tip.

> **CRAWL COLLÉ**—Divide the bow into 8 equal parts. Start at the tip, and play each stroke lower in the bow until you reach the frog. Then work back toward the tip again.

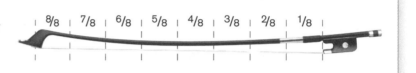

69 **LEARNING TO PLAY CRAWL COLLÉ**—*Prepare to play the* collé *stroke during the rests between notes.*

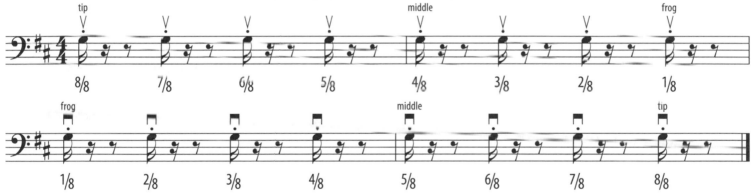

70 **SCALE CRAWL USING COLLÉ**—*Prepare to play the* collé *stroke during the rests between notes.*

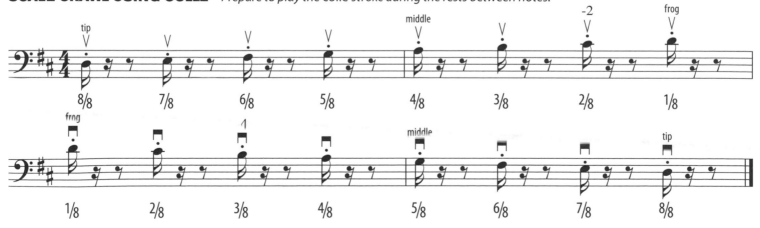

Level 2: Sound Bowings
Spiccato

SPICCATO–Separate bow strokes that bounce off the string, sometimes called a brush stroke. *Sound Advice:* Start on the string and gradually lift weight out of the bow allowing it to bounce in an arc-like motion (⌣) over the string.

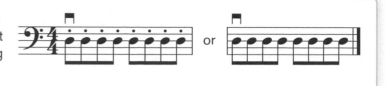

71 TAKING OFF—*Gradually lift weight out of the bow and shorten the stroke until the hair leaves the string and begins to bounce.*

72 LANDING—*Gradually lengthen the stroke and add weight to the bow until the hair stays on the string.*

73 ALTERNATING ON AND OFF THE STRING—*Practice letting the hair stay on and leave the string.*

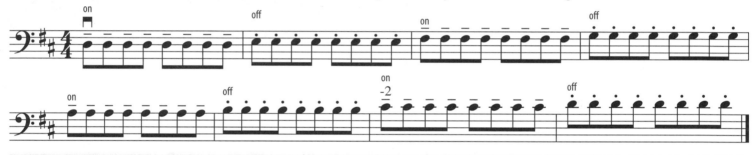

SPICCATO BOW PLACEMENTS

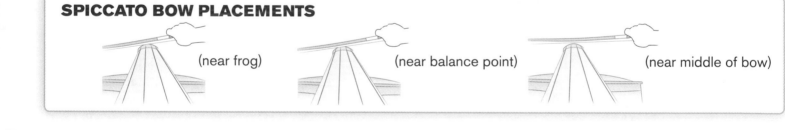

(near frog)　　(near balance point)　　(near middle of bow)

74 FARANDOLE—*Practice playing spiccato near the frog.*　　　Georges Bizet

75 CONTRADANSE—*Practice playing spiccato at the balance point.*　　　Antonio Salieri

76 THE MAGIC FLUTE—*Practice playing spiccato in the middle of the bow. Be careful to play the up-bow hooks with a spiccato bowing.*　　　Wolfgang Amadeus Mozart

Level 2: Sound Bowings
Chop

📹 **CHOP**—Indicates a percussive effect used as a rhythmic accompaniment with any number of patterns. *Sound Advice: The down-bow chop should dig into into the string and make an additional sound on the up bow.*

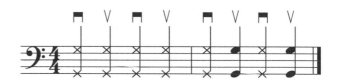

CHOPPING EXERCISE
1. Straighten your bow-hand thumb; roll the stick toward your face.
2. The bow should start close to the string.
3. Use wrist motion to slap the bow down with a slight motion toward the fingerboard (Violin/Viola) or bridge (Cello/Bass).
4. Pop the bow off the string with a slight upward motion that results in an additional sound.

77 **LEARNING TO CHOP**—*Using all the techniques learned above, chop on beats 2 and 4.*

78 **LEARNING TO CHOP AND DAMPEN**—*The up-bow chop is played by flicking the bow up using your right-hand wrist and fingers. Use your left-hand fingers to dampen (d) the strings just after the up bow.*

79 **CHOPPING AND PLAYING**—*Practice alternating between playing chop strokes and dampened quarter notes.*

80 **LEARNING TO CHANGE PITCHES WHILE CHOPPING**—*Practice changing your left-hand fingers while chopping.*

81 **MARI'S WEDDING MELODY**—*Play the melody to Mari's Wedding while your stand partner plays the chop accompaniment. Take turns performing the piece in small and large ensembles with your classmates. Take turns evaluating the performances using criteria you develop with your teacher.*

Irish Fiddle Tune

82 **MARI'S WEDDING CHOP ACCOMPANIMENT**—*Play the chop accompaniment to Mari's Wedding while your stand partner plays the melody.*

Irish Fiddle Tune

20

Level 3: Sound Shifting
Natural Harmonics

NATURAL HARMONICS occur when the string is touched lightly at the halfway point between the nut and the bridge so it vibrates on both sides of the finger. They can also occur at the point where the string is divided into three or four parts. The harmonic at the halfway point is usually notated $\frac{4}{0}$ for violins and violas and $\frac{3}{0}$ for cellos and basses.

SUL means "on the." *Sul* D indicates to play the notes on the D string.

Open D string

Harmonic D played *Sul* D (on the D string)

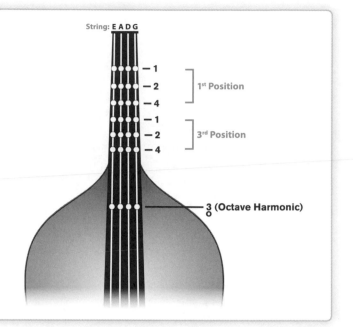

83 FINDING THE D HARMONIC—*Be careful to follow the fingerings.*

84 PLAYING THE D HARMONIC—*Be careful to follow the fingerings.*

85 PLAYING THE A HARMONIC—*Be careful to follow the fingerings.*

86 PLAYING THE G HARMONIC—*Be careful to follow the fingerings.*

87 PLAYING THE C HARMONIC—*Violas and cellos play the C harmonic while violins and basses review.*

88 PLAYING THE E HARMONIC—*Violins and basses play the E harmonic while violas and cellos review.*

Bass Fingering Chart

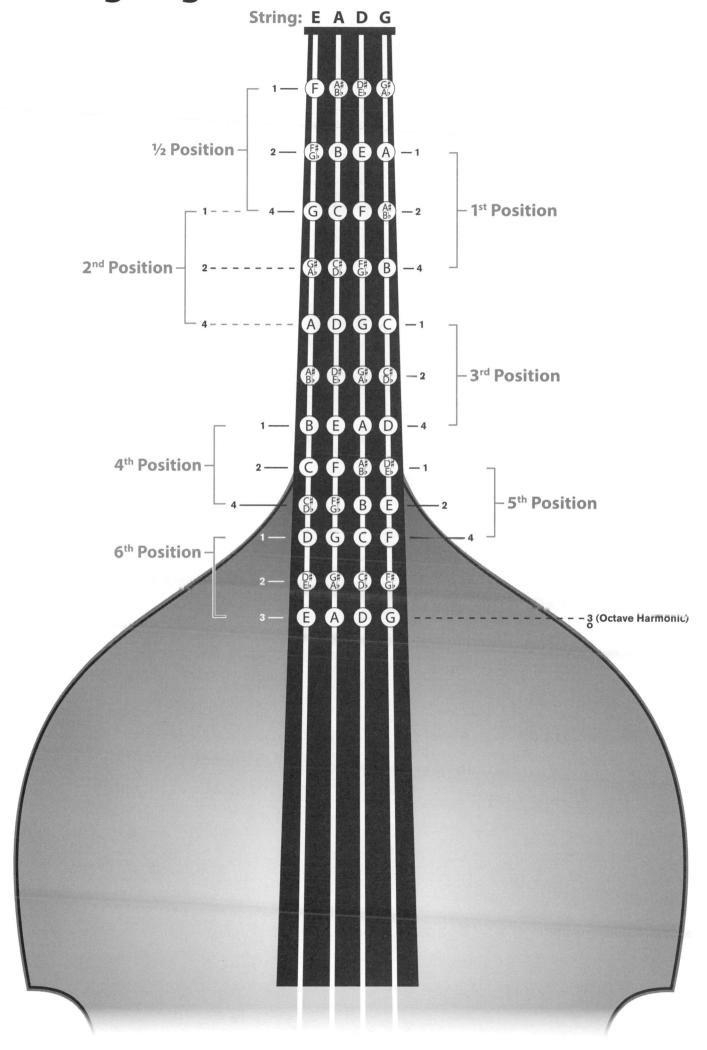

Level 3: Sound Shifting
Playing in 3rd Position: Using Pattern 1   ▶ *Shifting*
Check your fingering chart for the new finger placements.

89 FINDING 3rd POSITION ON THE D STRING USING PATTERN 1—*Violins and violas find notes in 3rd position. Cellos find notes in 3rd and 4th positions. Basses find notes in 3rd, 4th and 5th positions.*

90 PATTERN 1 ON THE D STRING IN 3rd POSITION—*Use the fingerings as marked.*

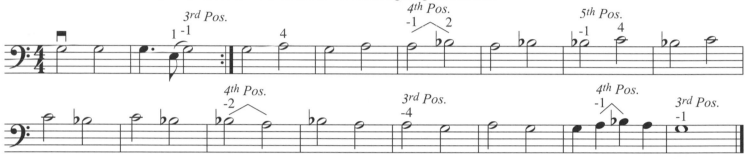

91 PATTERN 1 ON THE D STRING IN 3rd POSITION AGAIN—*Use the fingerings as marked. Basses play on the D and G strings.*

92 FINDING 3rd POSITION ON THE A STRING USING PATTERN 1—*Violins and violas find notes in 3rd position. Cellos find notes in 3rd and 4th positions. Basses find notes in 3rd, 4th and 5th positions.*

93 PATTERN 1 ON THE A STRING IN 3rd POSITION—*Use the fingerings as marked.*

94 PATTERN 1 ON THE A STRING IN 3rd POSITION AGAIN—*Use the fingerings as marked. Basses play on the A and D strings.*

Level 3: Sound Shifting
Playing in 3rd Position: Using Pattern 1
Check your fingering chart for the new finger placements.

95 **FINDING 3rd POSITION ON THE G STRING USING PATTERN 1**—*Violins and violas find notes in 3rd position. Cellos find notes in 3rd and 4th positions. Basses find notes in 3rd, 4th and 5th positions.*

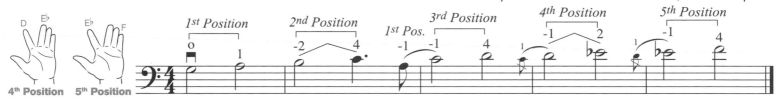

96 **PATTERN 1 ON THE G STRING IN 3rd POSITION**—*Use the fingerings as marked.*

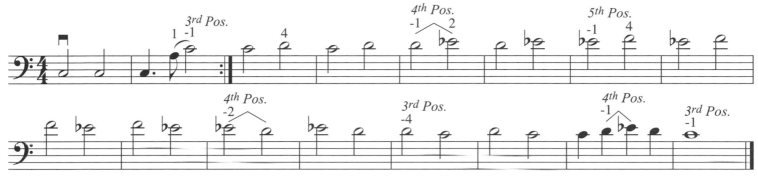

97 **PATTERN 1 ON THE G STRING IN 3rd POSITION AGAIN**—*Use the fingerings as marked. Basses play on the A and D strings.*

98 **FINDING 3rd POSITION ON THE E AND C STRINGS USING PATTERN 1**—*Violins and violas find notes in 3rd position. Cellos find notes in 3rd and 4th positions. Basses find notes in 3rd, 4th and 5th positions.*

99 **PATTERN 1 ON THE E AND C STRINGS IN 3rd POSITION**—*Use the fingerings as marked.*

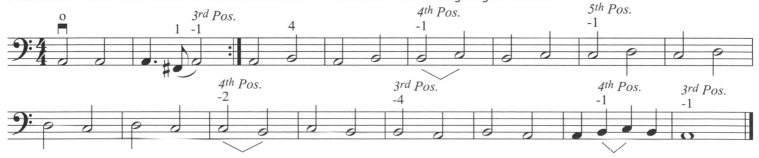

100 **PATTERN 1 ON THE E AND C STRINGS IN 3rd POSITION AGAIN**—*Use the fingerings as marked. Basses play on the A and D strings.*

Level 3: Sound Shifting
Playing in 3rd Position: Using Pattern 1

101 **LAS MAÑANITAS**—*Play Las Mañanitas in 3rd position using Pattern No. 1. Cellos and basses play in a variety of positions. Perform this piece for your friends and family using good left and right hand technique.*

Mexican Birthday Song

102 **CHESTER**—*Play Chester in 3rd position using Pattern No. 1. Cellos and basses play in a variety of positions. Challenge: Take turns performing Chester for your classmates. While listening, practice good concert etiquette.*

William Billings

Level 3: Sound Shifting
Shifting from 1st to 3rd Position

A **GUIDE/TRANSPORT FINGER** is the finger you use to shift from one position to another. It helps guide/transport you to the new position. *Sound Advice:* Just before the guide/transport finger is ready to move to the new position, release the weight in the finger as if you are playing a harmonic. Then smoothly move to the new position and reapply the finger weight.

103 **SHIFTING FROM 1st TO 3rd POSITION**—*Violins and violas practice shifting from 1st to 3rd position. Cellos and basses play in a variety of positions.*

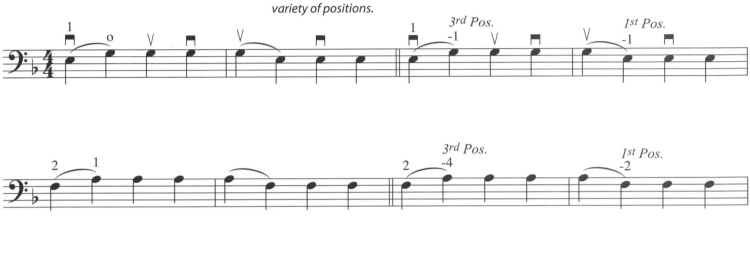

Level 3: Sound Shifting

Playing in 3rd Position: Using Pattern 2

Check your fingering chart for the new finger placements.

104 **FINDING 3rd POSITION ON THE D STRING USING PATTERN 2**—*Violins and violas find notes in 3rd position. Cellos find notes in 3rd and 4th positions. Basses find notes in 3rd, 3½ and 5th positions.*

105 **PATTERN 2 ON THE D STRING IN 3rd POSITION**—*Use the fingerings as marked. Cellos and basses play in a variety of positions.*

106 **PATTERN 2 ON THE D STRING IN 3rd POSITION AGAIN**—*Use the fingerings as marked. Cellos and basses play in a variety of positions.*

107 **FINDING 3rd POSITION ON THE A STRING USING PATTERN 2**—*Violins and violas find notes in 3rd position. Cellos find notes in 3rd and 4th positions. Basses find notes in 3rd, 3½ and 5th positions.*

108 **PATTERN 2 ON THE A STRING IN 3rd POSITION**—*Use the fingerings as marked. Cellos and basses play in a variety of positions.*

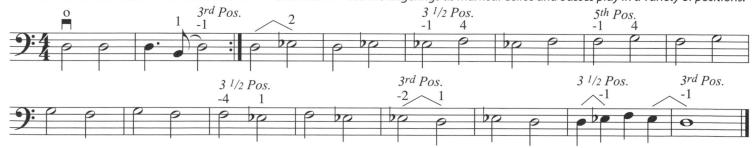

109 **PATTERN 2 ON THE A STRING IN 3rd POSITION AGAIN**—*Use the fingerings as marked. Cellos and basses play in a variety of positions.*

Level 3: Sound Shifting
Playing in 3rd Position: Using Pattern 2
Check your fingering chart for the new finger placements.

110 **FINDING 3rd POSITION ON THE G STRING USING PATTERN 2**—*Violins and violas find notes in 3rd position. Cellos find notes in 3rd and 4th positions. Basses find notes in 3rd, 3½ and 5th positions.*

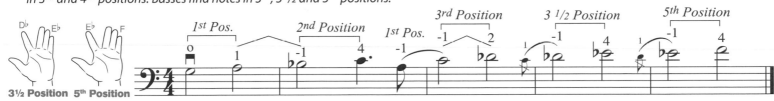

111 **PATTERN 2 ON THE G STRING IN 3rd POSITION**—*Use the fingerings as marked.*

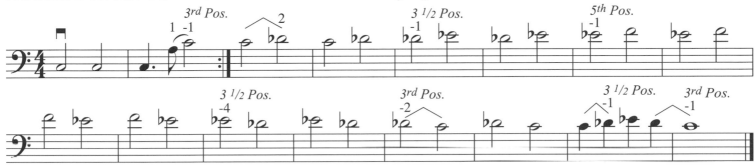

112 **PATTERN 2 ON THE G STRING IN 3rd POSITION AGAIN**—*Use the fingerings as marked. Basses review.*

113 **FINDING 3rd POSITION ON THE E AND C STRINGS USING PATTERN 2**—*Violins and violas find notes in 3rd position. Cellos find notes in 3rd and 4th positions. Basses find notes in 3rd, 3½ and 5th positions.*

114 **PATTERN 2 ON THE E AND C STRING IN 3rd POSITION**—*Use the fingerings as marked. Cellos and basses play in a variety of positions.*

115 **PATTERN 2 ON THE E AND C STRINGS IN 3rd POSITION AGAIN**—*Use the fingerings as marked.*

Level 3: Sound Shifting
Playing in 3rd Position: Using Pattern 3
Check your fingering chart for the new finger placements.

116 **FINDING 3rd POSITION ON THE D STRING USING PATTERN 3**—*Violins and violas find notes in 3rd position. Cellos find notes in 3rd and 4th positions. Basses find notes in 3rd, 4th and 5th positions.*

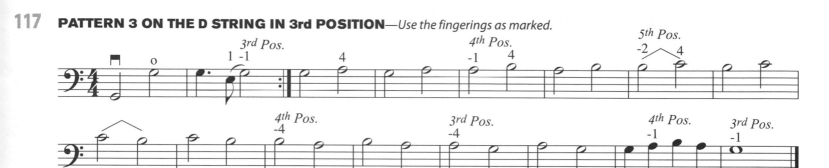

117 **PATTERN 3 ON THE D STRING IN 3rd POSITION**—*Use the fingerings as marked.*

118 **PATTERN 3 ON THE D STRING IN 3rd POSITION AGAIN**—*Use the fingerings as marked.*

119 **FINDING 3rd POSITION ON THE A STRING USING PATTERN 3**—*Violins and violas find notes in 3rd position. Cellos find notes in 3rd and 4th positions. Basses find notes in 3rd, 4th and 5th positions.*

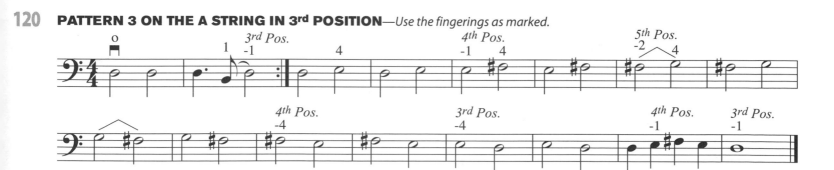

120 **PATTERN 3 ON THE A STRING IN 3rd POSITION**—*Use the fingerings as marked.*

121 **PATTERN 3 ON THE A STRING IN 3rd POSITION AGAIN**—*Use the fingerings as marked.*

Level 3: Sound Shifting
Playing in 3rd Position: Using Pattern 3
Check your fingering chart for the new finger placements.

122 **FINDING 3rd POSITION ON THE G STRING USING PATTERN 3**—*Violins and violas find notes in 3rd position. Cellos find notes in 3rd and 4th positions. Basses find notes in 3rd, 4th and 5th positions.*

123 **PATTERN 3 ON THE G STRING IN 3rd POSITION**—*Use the fingerings as marked.*

124 **PATTERN 3 ON THE G STRING IN 3rd POSITION AGAIN**—*Use the fingerings as marked.*

125 **FINDING 3rd POSITION ON THE E AND C STRINGS USING PATTERN 3**—*Violins and violas find notes in 3rd position. Cellos find notes in 3rd and 4th positions. Basses find notes in 3rd, 4th and 5th positions.*

126 **PATTERN 3 ON THE E AND C STRINGS IN 3rd POSITION**—*Use the fingerings as marked.*

127 **PATTERN 3 ON THE E AND C STRINGS IN 3rd POSITION AGAIN**—*Use the fingerings as marked.*

Level 3: Sound Shifting
Playing in 3ʳᵈ Position: Using Pattern 2

128   **THEME FROM VIOLIN CONCERTO**—*Violins and violas play* Theme from Violin Concerto *in 3ʳᵈ position using Pattern No. 2. Cellos use 3ʳᵈ and 4ᵗʰ positions. Basses use 2ⁿᵈ and 3 ½ positions.*

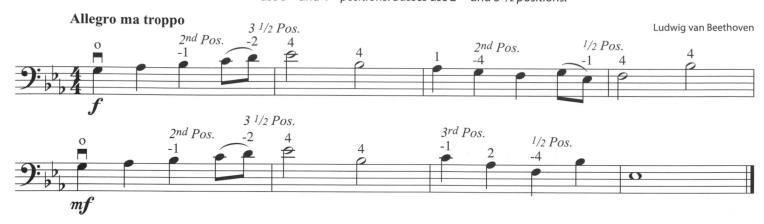

129   **MARCH FROM JUDAS MACCABEUS**—*Violins and violas play* Judas Maccabeus *in 3ʳᵈ position using Pattern No. 2. Cellos use 3ʳᵈ and 4ᵗʰ positions. Basses use 2ⁿᵈ and 3 ½ positions.*

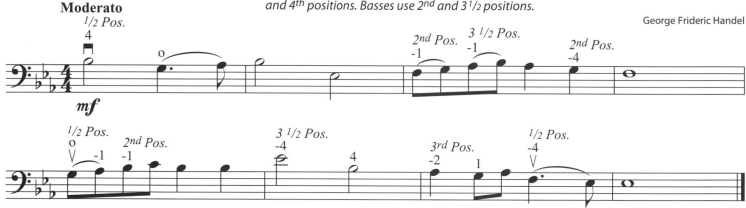

130   **AURA LEE**—*Violins and violas play* Aura Lee *in 3ʳᵈ position using Pattern No. 2. Before playing, mark the half steps using (ᴠ). Cellos use 3ʳᵈ and 4ᵗʰ positions. Basses use 3ʳᵈ, 4ᵗʰ and 5ᵗʰ positions. Challenge: Listen to a recording of this song and identify the number of sections. After playing the piece, circle the sections that are alike.*

Level 3: Sound Shifting
Shifting from 1st to 3rd Position

131 **LONG, LONG AGO**—*Violins and violas practice going from 1st to 3rd position. Cellos practice 3rd and 4th positions. Basses practice 2nd, 3rd and 4th positions. Challenge: Play* Long, Long Ago *from memory.*

Thomas Haynes Bayly

132 **SCOTTISH AIR**—*Violins and violas practice going from 1st to 3rd position. Cellos practice 3rd and 4th positions. Basses practice 2nd, 3rd, 4th and 5th positions. Challenge: Use all the sound variables from Level 1 to play* Scottish Air *expressively.*

Traditional

32

Level 3: Sound Shifting
Playing In 3rd Position: Using Pattern 3
Check your fingering chart for the new finger placements.

133 **THEME FROM SERENADE FOR STRINGS**—*Violins and violas play* Theme from Serenade for Strings *in 3rd position using Pattern No. 3. Cellos play in 3rd and 4th positions. Basses play in 2nd, 3rd, 4th and 5th positions.*

Pyotr Ilyich Tchaikovsky

134 **THEME FROM SYMPHONY No. 9**—*Violins and violas play* Theme from Symphony No. 9 *in 3rd position using Pattern No. 3. Cellos play in 3rd position. Basses play in 3rd and 4th positions.*

Antonín Dvořák

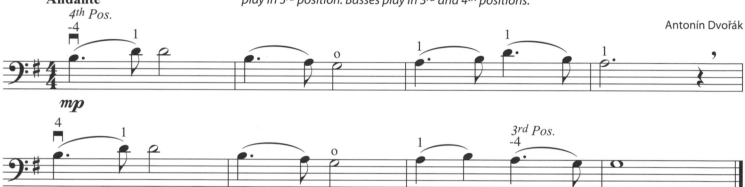

135 **THEME FROM ROSAMUNDE**—*Violins and violas play* Theme from Rosamunde *in 3rd position using Pattern No. 3. Cellos play in 3rd and 4th positions. Basses play in 3rd, 4th and 5th positions.*

Franz Schubert

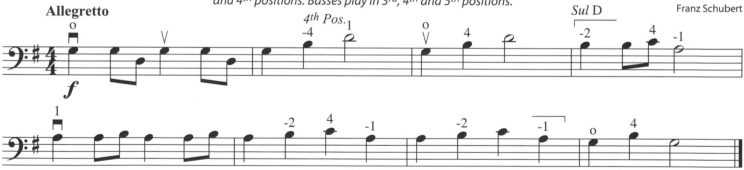

136 **ALLELUIA**—*Violins and violas play* Alleluia *in 3rd position using Pattern No. 3. Cellos play in 3rd and 4th positions. Basses play in 3rd, 4th and 5th positions.*

Wolfgang Amadeus Mozart

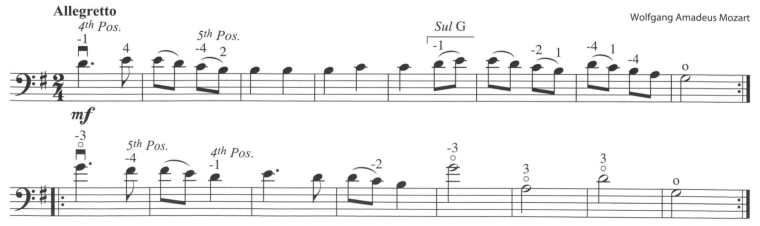

Level 3: Sound Shifting
Playing In 2nd Position: Using Pattern 3
Check your fingering chart for the new finger placements.

137 **FINDING 2nd POSITION ON THE D STRING USING PATTERN 3**—*Violins and violas find notes in 2nd position. Cellos find notes in 2nd and 3rd positions. Basses find notes in 2nd, 3rd and 4th positions.*

138 **MORE PLAYING IN 2nd POSITION**—*Be careful to follow all fingerings.*

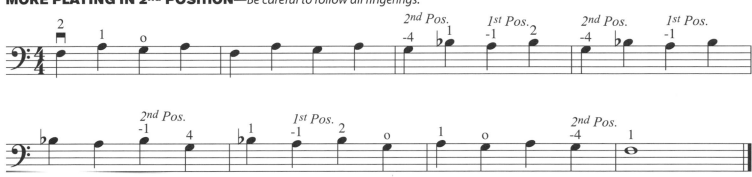

139 **MATTACHINS (SWORD DANCE)**—*Play Sword Dance using 2nd position.*

Renaissance Dance

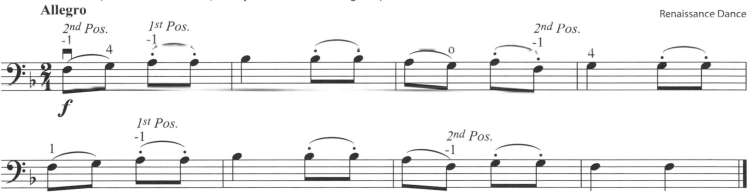

140 **ETUDE**—*Write the fingerings over each note that can be played in 2nd position.*

Charles de Beriot

Level 3: Sound Shifting
Playing In 4th Position: Using Pattern 1
Check your fingering chart for the new finger placements.

141 **FINDING 4th POSITION ON THE D STRING USING PATTERN No. 1**—*Practice finding 4th position. Basses play in 4th and 6th positions.*

142 **LEARNING TO PLAY IN 4th POSITION**—*Learn to play in 4th position. Basses play in 4th, 5th and 6th positions.*

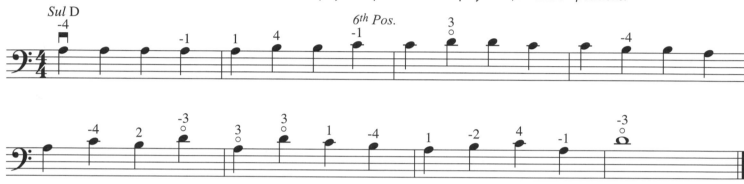

143 **PERPETUAL MOTION IN 4th POSITION**—*Be careful to follow all fingerings. Cellos and basses review.*
Challenge: Write in the remaining fingerings.

Traditional

144 **PLAYING IN 4th POSITION**—*Practice playing in 4th position. Basses play in 4th, 5th and 6th positions.*

Level 3: Sound Shifting
Playing In 5ᵗʰ Position: Using Pattern 3

Check your fingering chart for the new finger placements.

145 **FINDING 5ᵗʰ POSITION ON THE D STRING USING PATTERN No. 3**—*Practice finding 5ᵗʰ position.*

146 **5ᵗʰ POSITION ON THE D STRING**—*Violin and viola 5ᵗʰ position fingerings can be read as if they were in 1ˢᵗ position one string higher.*

147 **5ᵗʰ POSITION ON THE A STRING**—*Violin and viola 5ᵗʰ position fingerings can be read as if they were in 1ˢᵗ position one string higher. Cellos and basses review.*

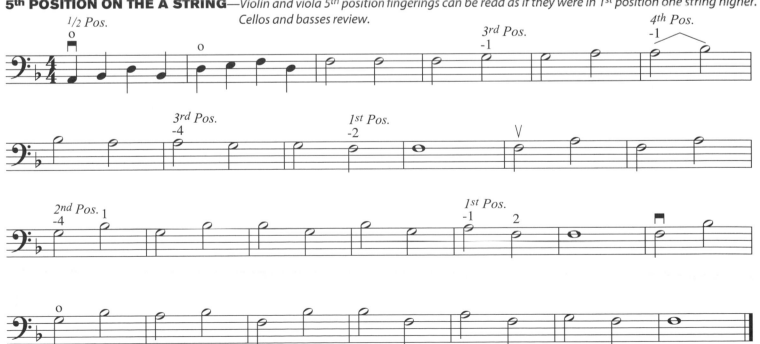

Level 3: Sound Shifting
Playing In 5th Position: Using Pattern 3

Check your fingering chart for the new finger placements.

148 **5th POSITION ON THE VIOLIN E STRING**—*Violin 5th position fingerings can be read as if they were in 1st position one string higher. Violas and cellos review.*

149 **5th POSITION WORKOUT**—*Practice playing in 5th position on the D and A strings. Cellos and basses review.*

Level 3: Sound Shifting
Shifting from 3rd to 5th Position

150 **SHIFTING FROM 3rd TO 5th POSITION ON THE A STRING**—*Be careful to follow all fingerings. Violins and violas practice going from 3rd to 5th position. Cellos and basses reveiw.*

151 **SHIFTING FROM 3rd TO 5th POSITION ON THE VIOLIN E STRING**—*Be careful to follow all fingerings. Violins practice going from 3rd to 5th position. Violas, cellos and basses reveiw.*

Level 3: Sound Shifting
Vibrato

PREPARING FOR VIBRATO

1. **FINGER ROCKERS**–Place your left-hand 2nd finger in the channel between your 3rd and 4th finger bones. Gently rock your finger up and down your hand.

2. **FINGER SHOOTS**–Lightly place your left-hand 2nd finger on the D string. Move up and down the string as if you are wiping off the dust. Gradually go faster and faster from 1st position to the top of the fingerboard.

3. **BOUT VIBRATO**–Place your 2nd finger on the D string and shift your left hand until it rests on the bout. Gently rock your 2nd finger up and down the string so your left hand bounces off the bout. The vibrato motion starts in the forearm.

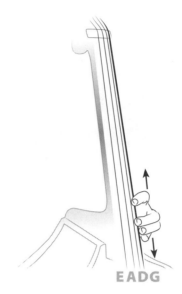

E A D G

VIBRATO is a slight fluctuation of the pitch below and above the written note. The vibrato finger rocks back and forth rapidly around the center point of the pitch to create a beautiful sound. The left hand will look like it shakes back and forth. Vibrato will warm the sound.

ROLLING THE FINGER BACKWARD–Gently roll the finger from the A to slightly below the A.

ROLLING THE FINGER FORWARD–Gently roll the finger from the A to slightly above the A.

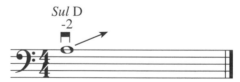

A BACKWARD VIBRATO MOTION–Gently roll the finger from the A to slightly below the A and back to the A.

A FORWARD VIBRATO MOTION–Gently roll the finger from the A to slightly above the A and back to the A.

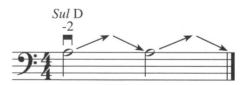

Level 3: Sound Shifting
Vibrato

152 **A COMPLETE VIBRATO MOTION**—*Starting on the note A, roll the finger backward and forward pulsing on each rhythm below.*

153 **THE G MAJOR SCALE STARTING AND STOPPING VIBRATO**—*Play the the first note of every measure with* vibrato *and the second note without* vibrato.

154 **CHESTER WITH VIBRATO**—*Play Chester using vibrato.*

William Billings

Level 4: Sound Scales, Arpeggios, Chorales & Rhythms

C Major   🎥 ▶ *Scales*

155   **C MAJOR SCALE**—*Use the fingerings above the notes or the alternate fingerings below the notes and play as directed by your teacher.**

A. *1st octave going up.*

2nd Pos.

B. *2nd octave going up. Basses repeat the 1st octave.*

C. *2nd octave going down. Basses repeat the 1st octave.*
2nd Pos.

1st Pos.

D. *1st octave going down.*

156   **C MAJOR ARPEGGIO**—*Play as directed by your teacher.*

A. *1st octave going up.*

B. *2nd octave going up. Basses repeat the 1st octave.*

C. *2nd octave going down. Basses repeat the 1st octave.*

D. *1st octave going down.*

157   **C MAJOR SCALE IN THIRDS**—*Play as directed by your teacher.*

A. *1st octave going up.*

B. *2nd octave going up. Basses repeat the 1st octave.*

C. *2nd octave going down. Basses repeat the 1st octave.*

D. *1st octave going down.*

158   **C MAJOR BOWING VARIATIONS**—*Play the C major scale using the bowing variations below.*

A.

B.

159   **C MAJOR SCALE ACCOMPANIMENTS**—*Take turns accompanying the scale above using either the harmonized or drone accompaniment.*

A. Harmonized Accompaniment—*Play repeats for two octave scales only.*

B. Drone Accompaniment—*Repeat throughout the scale.*

Challenge: Listen to the ensemble as the class plays the scale and accompaniment together. Aurally identify which part is the scale and which part is the accompaniment.

* *Basses have one set of fingerings for each scale.*

Level 4: Sound Scales, Arpeggios, Chorales & Rhythms
A Natural Minor

160

A NATURAL MINOR SCALE—*Use the fingerings above the notes or the alternate fingerings below the notes and play as directed by your teacher.*

A. *1st octave going up.*

B. *2nd octave going up. Basses repeat the 1st octave.*

C. *2nd octave going down. Basses repeat the 1st octave.*

D. *1st octave going down.*

161

A NATURAL MINOR ARPEGGIO—*Play as directed by your teacher.*

A. *1st octave going up.*

B. *2nd octave going up. Basses repeat the 1st octave.*

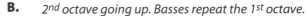

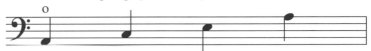

C. *2nd octave going down. Basses repeat the 1st octave.*

D. *1st octave going down.*

162

A NATURAL MINOR SCALE IN THIRDS—*Play as directed by your teacher.*

A. *1st octave going up.*

B. *2nd octave going up. Basses repeat the 1st octave.*

C. *2nd octave going down. Basses repeat the 1st octave.*

D. *1st octave going down.*

163

A NATURAL MINOR BOWING VARIATIONS—*Play the A natural minor scale using the bowing variations below.*

A.

B.

164

A NATURAL MINOR SCALE ACCOMPANIMENTS—*Take turns accompanying the scale above using either the harmonized or drone accompaniment.*

A. Harmonized Accompaniment—*Play repeats for two octave scales only.*

B. Drone Accompaniment—*Repeat throughout the scale.*

Challenge: Identify the intervals being used in the A Natural Minor Arpeggio exercise.

Level 4: Sound Scales, Arpeggios, Chorales & Rhythms
G Major

165 **G MAJOR SCALE**—*Use the fingerings above the notes or the alternate fingerings below the notes and play as directed by your teacher.*

A. *1st octave going up.*

B. *2nd octave going up.*

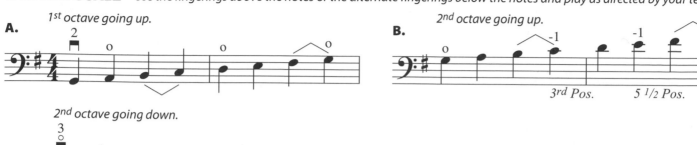

3rd Pos.   *5 1/2 Pos.*

C. *2nd octave going down.*

D. *1st octave going down.*

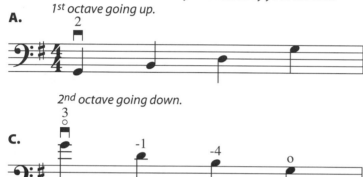

5 1/2 Pos.   *3rd Pos.*   *1st Pos.*

166 **G MAJOR ARPEGGIO**—*Play as directed by your teacher.*

A. *1st octave going up.*

B. *2nd octave going up.*

C. *2nd octave going down.*

D. *1st octave going down.*

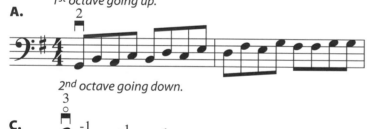

167 **G MAJOR SCALE IN THIRDS**—*Play as directed by your teacher.*

A. *1st octave going up.*

B. *2nd octave going up.*

C. *2nd octave going down.*

D. *1st octave going down.*

168 **G MAJOR BOWING VARIATIONS**—*Play the G major scale using the bowing variations below.*

A.

B.

169 **G MAJOR SCALE ACCOMPANIMENTS**—*Take turns accompanying the scale above using either the harmonized or drone accompaniment.*

A. Harmonized Accompaniment—*Play repeats for two octave scales only.*

B. Drone Accompaniment—*Repeat throughout the scale.*

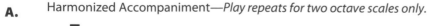
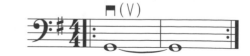

Challenge: Identify which part of the chord you are playing on each quarter note in the harmonized accompaniment.

Level 4: Sound Scales, Arpeggios, Chorales & Rhythms
E Natural Minor

170 **E NATURAL MINOR SCALE**—*Use the fingerings above the notes or the alternate fingerings below the notes and play as directed by your teacher.*

A. *1st octave going up.*

B. *2nd octave going up.*

C. *2nd octave going down.*

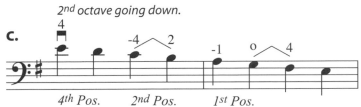

D. *1st octave going down.*

171 **E NATURAL MINOR ARPEGGIO**—*Play as directed by your teacher.*

A. *1st octave going up.*

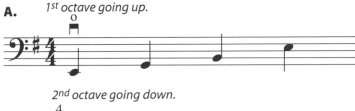

B. *2nd octave going up.*

C. *2nd octave going down.*

D. *1st octave going down.*

172 **E NATURAL MINOR SCALE IN THIRDS**—*Play as directed by your teacher.*

A. *1st octave going up.*

B. *2nd octave going up.*

C. *2nd octave going down.*

D. *1st octave going down.*

173 **E NATURAL MINOR BOWING VARIATIONS**—*Play the E natural minor scale using the bowing variations below.*

A.

B.

174 **E NATURAL MINOR SCALE ACCOMPANIMENTS**—*Take turns accompanying the scale above using either the harmonized or drone accompaniment.*

A. Harmonized Accompaniment—*Play repeats for two octave scales only.*

B. Drone Accompaniment— *Repeat throughout the scale.*

Challenge: By ear, indentify each interval you play while using the drone accompaniment with the scale.

Level 4: Sound Scales, Arpeggios, Chorales & Rhythms
D Major

175 **D MAJOR SCALE**—*Use the fingerings above the notes or the alternate fingerings below the notes and play as directed by your teacher.*

A. *1st octave going up.*

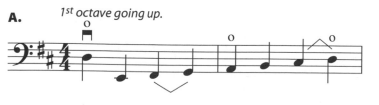

B. *2nd octave going up.*

3rd Pos.

C. *2nd octave going down.*

3rd Pos. *1st Pos.*

D. *1st octave going down.*

176 **D MAJOR ARPEGGIO**—*Play as directed by your teacher.*

A. *1st octave going up.*

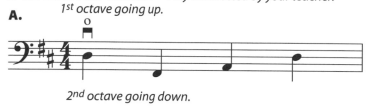

B. *2nd octave going up.*

C. *2nd octave going down.*

D. *1st octave going down.*

177 **D MAJOR SCALE IN THIRDS**—*Play as directed by your teacher.*

A. *1st octave going up.*

B. *2nd octave going up.*

C. *2nd octave going down.*

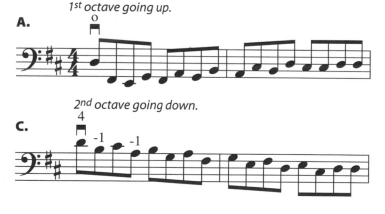

D. *1st octave going down.*

178 **D MAJOR BOWING VARIATIONS**—*Play the D major scale using the bowing variations below.*

A.

B.

179 **D MAJOR SCALE ACCOMPANIMENTS**—*Take turns accompanying the scale above using either the harmonized or drone accompaniment.*

A. Harmonized Accompaniment—*Play repeats for two octave scales only.*

B. Drone Accompaniment— *Repeat throughout the scale.*

Challenge: Record yourself playing the D major scale and evalute your performance for intonation.

Level 4: Sound Scales, Arpeggios, Chorales & Rhythms
B Natural Minor

180 **B NATURAL MINOR SCALE**—*Use the fingerings above the notes or the alternate fingerings below the notes and play as directed by your teacher.*

A. *1st octave going up.*

B. *2nd octave going up. Basses repeat the 1st octave.*

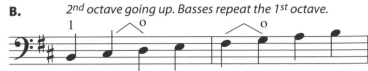

C. *2nd octave going down. Basses repeat the 1st octave.*

D. *1st octave going down.*

181 **B NATURAL MINOR ARPEGGIO**—*Play as directed by your teacher.*

A. *1st octave going up.*

B. *2nd octave going up. Basses repeat the 1st octave.*

C. *2nd octave going down. Basses repeat the 1st octave.*

D. *1st octave going down.*

182 **B NATURAL MINOR SCALE IN THIRDS**—*Play as directed by your teacher.*

A. *1st octave going up.*

B. *2nd octave going up. Basses repeat the 1st octave.*

C. *2nd octave going down. Basses repeat the 1st octave.*

D. *1st octave going down.*

183 **B NATURAL MINOR BOWING VARIATIONS**—*Play the B natural minor scale using the bowing variations below.*

A.

B.

184 **B NATURAL MINOR SCALE ACCOMPANIMENTS**—*Take turns accompanying the scale above using either the harmonized or drone accompaniment.*

A. Harmonized Accompaniment—*Play repeats for two octave scales only.*

B. Drone Accompaniment—*Repeat throughout the scale.*

Challenge: Record yourself playing the B natural minor scale and evaluate your performance for rhythmic stability.

Level 4: Sound Scales, Arpeggios, Chorales & Rhythms
A Major

185 **A MAJOR SCALE**—*Use the fingerings above the notes or the alternate fingerings below the notes and play as directed by your teacher.*

A. *1st octave going up.*

B. *2nd octave going up. Basses repeat the 1st octave.*

C. *2nd octave going down. Basses repeat the 1st octave.*

D. *1st octave going down.*

186 **A MAJOR ARPEGGIO**—*Play as directed by your teacher.*

A. *1st octave going up.*
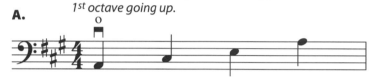

B. *2nd octave going up. Basses repeat the 1st octave.*

C. *2nd octave going down. Basses repeat the 1st octave.*
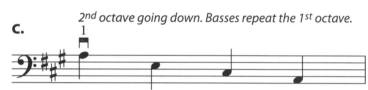

D. *1st octave going down.*
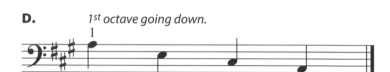

187 **A MAJOR SCALE IN THIRDS**—*Play as directed by your teacher.*

A. *1st octave going up.*

B. *2nd octave going up. Basses repeat the 1st octave.*
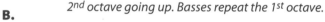

C. *2nd octave going down. Basses repeat the 1st octave.*

D. *1st octave going down.*

188 **A MAJOR BOWING VARIATIONS**—*Play the A major scale using the bowing variations below.*

A.

B.

189 **A MAJOR SCALE ACCOMPANIMENTS**—*Take turns accompanying the scale above using either the harmonized or drone accompaniment.*

A. Harmonized Accompaniment—*Play repeats for two octave scales only.*

B. Drone Accompaniment—*Repeat throughout the scale.*

Challenge: Perform the A major scale in a round with your stand partner and listen for good intonation.

Level 4: Sound Scales, Arpeggios, Chorales & Rhythms
F Major

190 **F MAJOR SCALE**—*Use the fingerings above the notes or the alternate fingerings below the notes and play as directed by your teacher.*

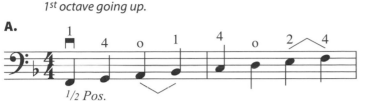

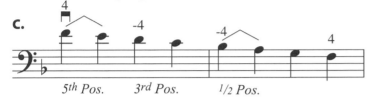

191 **F MAJOR ARPEGGIO**—*Play as directed by your teacher.*

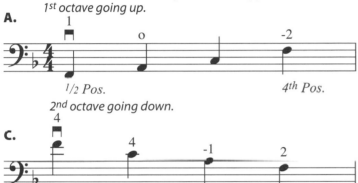

192 **F MAJOR SCALE IN THIRDS**—*Play as directed by your teacher.*

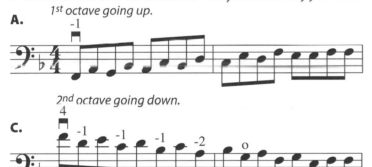

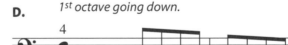

193 **F MAJOR BOWING VARIATIONS**—*Play the F major scale using the bowing variations below.*

194 **F MAJOR SCALE ACCOMPANIMENTS**—*Take turns accompanying the scale above using either the harmonized or drone accompaniment.*

Challenge: Play the F major scale and arpeggio from memory.

Level 4: Sound Scales, Arpeggios, Chorales & Rhythms
D Natural Minor

195 **D NATURAL MINOR SCALE**—*Use the fingerings above the notes or the alternate fingerings below the notes and play as directed by your teacher.*

A. *1st octave going up.*

B. *2nd octave going up.*

C. *2nd octave going down.*

D. *1st octave going down.*

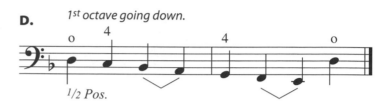

196 **D NATURAL MINOR ARPEGGIO**—*Play as directed by your teacher.*

A. *1st octave going up.*

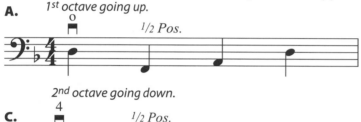

B. *2nd octave going up.*

C. *2nd octave going down.*

D. *1st octave going down.*

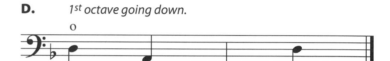

197 **D NATURAL MINOR SCALE IN THIRDS**—*Play as directed by your teacher.*

A. *1st octave going up.*

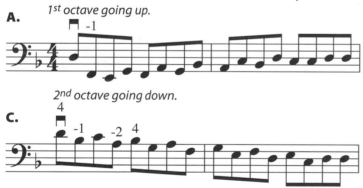

B. *2nd octave going up.*

C. *2nd octave going down.*

D. *1st octave going down.*

198 **D NATURAL MINOR BOWING VARIATIONS**—*Play the D natural minor scale using the bowing variations below.*

A.

B.

199 **D NATURAL MINOR SCALE ACCOMPANIMENTS**—*Take turns accompanying the scale above using either the harmonized or drone accompaniment.*

A. Harmonized Accompaniment—*Play repeats for two octave scales only.*

Drone Accompaniment—
Repeat throughout the scale.

B.

Challenge: Play the D natural minor scale with a metronome. Start at a slow tempo and work to a faster tempo.

Level 4: Sound Scales, Arpeggios, Chorales & Rhythms
B♭ Major

200 **B♭ MAJOR SCALE**—*Use the fingerings above the notes or the alternate fingerings below the notes and play as directed by your teacher.*

1st octave going up.

A.

2nd octave going up. Basses repeat the 1st octave.

B.

2nd octave going down. Basses repeat the 1st octave.

C.

1st octave going down.

D.

201 **B♭ MAJOR ARPEGGIO**—*Play as directed by your teacher.*

1st octave going up.

A.

2nd octave going up. Basses repeat the 1st octave.

B.

2nd octave going down. Basses repeat the 1st octave.

C.

1st octave going down.

D.

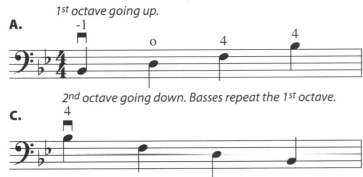

202 **B♭ MAJOR SCALE IN THIRDS**—*Play as directed by your teacher.*

1st octave going up.

A.

2nd octave going up. Basses repeat the 1st octave.

B.

2nd octave going down. Basses repeat the 1st octave.

C.

1st octave going down.

D.

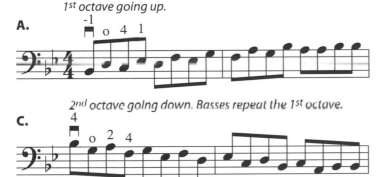

203 **B♭ MAJOR BOWING VARIATIONS**—*Play the B♭ major scale using the bowing variations below.*

A.

B.

204 **B♭ MAJOR SCALE ACCOMPANIMENTS**—*Take turns accompanying the scale above using either the harmonized or drone accompaniment.*

A. Harmonized Accompaniment—*Play repeats for two octave scales only.*

B. Drone Accompaniment— *Repeat throughout the scale.*

Challenge: Take turns playing the B♭ Major Scale In Thirds and the Drone Accompaniment with your stand partner. Listen for good intonation.

Level 4: Sound Scales, Arpeggios, Chorales & Rhythms
G Natural Minor

205 **G NATURAL MINOR SCALE**—*Use the fingerings above the notes or the alternate fingerings below the notes and play as directed by your teacher.*

1st octave going up.

A.

½ Pos.

2nd octave going up.

B.

3rd Pos.   *5th Pos.*

2nd octave going down.

C.

5th Pos.   *3rd Pos.*   *½ Pos.*

D. *1st octave going down.*

206 **G NATURAL MINOR ARPEGGIO**—*Play as directed by your teacher.*

A. *1st octave going up.*

B. *2nd octave going up.*

2nd octave going down.

C.

D. *1st octave going down.*

207 **G NATURAL MINOR SCALE IN THIRDS**—*Play as directed by your teacher.*

A. *1st octave going up.*

B. *2nd octave going up.*

2nd octave going down.

C.

D. *1st octave going down.*

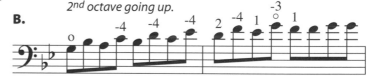

208 **G NATURAL MINOR BOWING VARIATIONS**—*Play the G natural minor scale using the bowing variations below.*

A.

B.

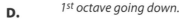

209 **G NATURAL MINOR SCALE ACCOMPANIMENTS**—*Take turns accompanying the scale above using either the harmonized or drone accompaniment.*

A. Harmonized Accompaniment—*Play repeats for two octave scales only.*

Drone Accompaniment—
Repeat throughout the scale.

B.

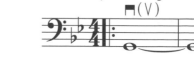

Challenge: Play the G natural minor scale using bowing patterns from some of the other scales.

Level 4: Sound Scales, Arpeggios, Chorales & Rhythms
E♭ Major

210 E♭ **MAJOR SCALE**—*Use the fingerings above the notes or alternate fingerings below the notes and play as directed by your teacher.*

A. *1st octave going up.*
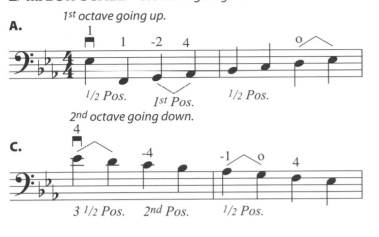

B. *2nd octave going up.*

C. *2nd octave going down.*

D. *1st octave going down.*
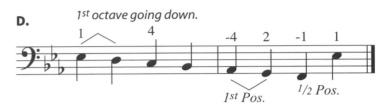

211 E♭ **MAJOR ARPEGGIO**—*Play as directed by your teacher.*

A. *1st octave going up.*

B. *2nd octave going up.*

C. *2nd octave going down.*

D. *1st octave going down.*

212 E♭ **MAJOR SCALE IN THIRDS**—*Play as directed by your teacher.*

A. *1st octave going up.*

B. *2nd octave going up.*

C. *2nd octave going down.*

D. *1st octave going down.*

213 E♭ **MAJOR BOWING VARIATIONS**—*Play the E♭ major scale using the bowing variations below.*

A.

B.

214 E♭ **MAJOR SCALE ACCOMPANIMENTS**—*Take turns accompanying the scale above using either the harmonized or drone accompaniment.*

A. Harmonized Accompaniment—*Play repeats for two octave scales only.*

B. Drone Accompaniment—*Repeat throughout the scale.*

Challenge: Take turns playing the E♭ major scale holding each note as a whole note while your stand partner plays the drone accompaniment. Listen carefully for good intonation.

Level 4: Sound Scales, Arpeggios, Chorales & Rhythms
Major Scales

215 **C MAJOR SCALE**—*Play as directed by your teacher.*

216 **G MAJOR SCALE**—*Play as directed by your teacher.*

217 **D MAJOR SCALE**—*Play as directed by your teacher.*

218 **A MAJOR SCALE**—*Play as directed by your teacher.*

219 **F MAJOR SCALE**—*Play as directed by your teacher.*

220 **B♭ MAJOR SCALE**—*Play as directed by your teacher.*

221 **E♭ MAJOR SCALE**—*Play as directed by your teacher.*

Level 4: Sound Scales, Arpeggios, Chorales & Rhythms
Minor Scales

222 **A NATURAL MINOR SCALE**—*Play as directed by your teacher.*

223 **E NATURAL MINOR SCALE**—*Play as directed by your teacher.*

224 **B NATURAL MINOR SCALE**—*Play as directed by your teacher.*

225 **D NATURAL MINOR SCALE**—*Play as directed by your teacher.*

226 **G NATURAL MINOR SCALE**—*Play as directed by your teacher.*

SIGHT-READING CHECKLIST

1. **TITLE**—check the title for information about the style or form of the piece.
2. **COMPOSER'S NAME**—check the composer's name for information about the style.
3. **TEMPOS AND TEMPO CHANGES**—check for information about the speed of the piece.
4. **KEY SIGNATURE AND KEY SIGNATURE CHANGES**—look for changes in the naturals, sharps, and flats.
5. **TIME SIGNATURE AND TIME SIGNATURE CHANGES**—check to see the number of beats in each measure and any changes.
6. **TRAFFIC PATTERNS**—check for information that indicates where to go in the music such as D.C., D.S. and repeats.
7. **DYNAMICS**—scan the piece for dynamics. Notice the beginning and ending dynamic.
8. **ACCIDENTALS**—scan the piece for accidentals.
9. **ARTICULATIONS**—scan the piece for articulations.
10. **BOWINGS**—scan the piece for special bowings and bowing patterns.
11. **POSITIONS AND FINGERINGS**—scan the piece for higher positions and finger pattern changes.

227 **SIGHT-READ IT**—*Scan the piece for each sight-reading checkpoint and then play. Evaluate your performance and decide how to improve it.*

Challenge: Use the sight-reading checklist to prepare to sight-read a piece your teacher chooses.

Level 4: Sound Scales, Arpeggios, Chorales & Rhythms
Finger Action

228 CHROMATIC MOVEMENT—*Violins and violas practice sliding a finger from one half step to another with precision. Cellos and basses review chromatic alterations.*

229 CHROMATIC SCALE—*Practice playing a chromatic scale. Challenge: Play the alternate fingerings.*

230 HORIZONTAL MOVEMENT—*Practice moving your finger horizontally from one string to the other. Lift the finger up. Basses review.*

231 VELOCITY EXERCISE—*Practice lifting your left-hand fingers like a spring.*

232 TRILL MOTION—*Practice the trill motion by alternating between two notes with faster and faster rhythms.*

233 TRILL EXERCISE—*Practice going between the written out trill motion and the trill notation.*

234 INDEPENDENT FINGER MOVEMENT—*Violins and violas practice moving fingers independently from each other while cellos and basses reveiw.*

Level 4: Sound Scales, Arpeggios, Chorales & Rhythms
Chorales

235 **CHORALE NO. 1, CHRISTUS, DER IST MEIN LEBEN**—*Listen to all parts and adjust your intonation to the other players. Your teacher will tell you whether to play Part A, the melody, or Part B, the accompaniment.*

Johann Sebastian Bach

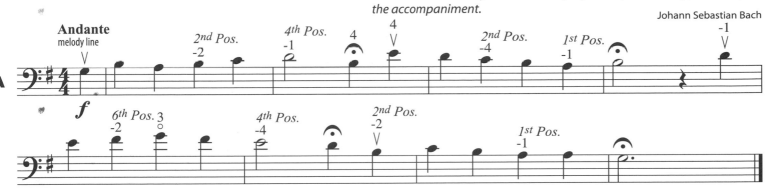

LEARN TO READ COMBINED PART NOTATION
Sometimes two separate parts are combined on one staff. Outside players perform the notes with stems up and inside players play the notes with the stems down.

236 **CHORALE NO. 2, RHOSYMEDRE**—*Listen to all parts and adjust your intonation to the other players. Your teacher will tell you whether to play the upper part, the melody, or the lower part, the accompaniment. Write in the fingerings for the upper notes above the staff and the lower notes below the staff.*

Jonathan David Edwards

Level 4: Sound Scales, Arpeggios, Chorales & Rhythms
Rhythms
Play each exercise on a note of your teacher's choice.

237 $\frac{4}{4}$ **RHYTHMS**—*Count, clap and play using a counting system of your teacher's choice. Play as a two-part round starting in a measure your teacher directs. Challenge: Compose, notate and perform your own rhythm patterns in this meter.*

238 $\frac{3}{4}$ **RHYTHMS**—*Count, clap and play using a counting system of your teacher's choice. Challenge: Compose a rhythmic accompaniment to this exercise. Create an arrangement by assigning instruments to play either the exercise or accompaniment, then play in a three-part round and assign instruments to each part.*

239 $\frac{5}{4}$ **RHYTHMS**—*Count, clap and play using a counting system of your teacher's choice. Play as a two-part round starting in a measure your teacher directs. Challenge: Improvise your own rhythm patterns in this meter.*

240 $\frac{2}{4}$ **RHYTHMS**—*Count, clap and play using a counting system of your teacher's choice. Play as a four-part round starting in a measure your teacher directs. Challenge: Improvise your own rhythm patterns in this meter.*

241 **CUT TIME RHYTHMS**—*Count, clap and play using a counting system of your teacher's choice. Play as a four-part round starting in a measure your teacher directs. Challenge: Improvise your own rhythm patterns in this meter.*

242 $\frac{6}{8}$ **RHYTHMS**—*Count, clap and play using a counting system of your teacher's choice. Challenge: Play by ear an eight bar phrase of $\frac{6}{8}$ rhythms from any $\frac{6}{8}$ piece you know. Play by ear an eight bar phrase from different genres of music in $\frac{6}{8}$ time.*

243 $\frac{9}{8}$ **RHYTHMS**—*Count, clap and play using a counting system of your teacher's choice. Take turns playing the $\frac{9}{8}$ rhythms for your stand partner and then evaluate the quality and effectiveness of your performances.*

244 $\frac{5}{8}$ **RHYTHMS**—*Count, clap and play using a counting system of your teacher's choice. Challenge: Write and perform your own rhythm patterns in this meter.*

245 $\frac{7}{8}$ **RHYTHMS**—*Count, clap and play using a counting system of your teacher's choice. Challenge: Write and perform your own rhythm patterns in this meter.*